ON CLEAVING TO GOD

St. Albertus Magnus

Translated: John Richards
Edited by: D.P. Curtin

Dalcassian Publishing Company

PHILADELPHIA, PA

Library of Congress Cataloging-in-Publication Data

Copyright © 2019 Dalcassian Publishing Co.
In association with St. Macartan Press

On the highest and supreme perfection of man, in so far as it is possible in this life
De ultima et summa perfectione hominis, quantum in hac vita possibile est.

I have had the idea of writing something for myself on and about the state of complete and full abstraction from everything and of cleaving freely, confidently, nakedly and firmly to God alone, so as to describe it fully (in so far as it is possible in this abode of exile and pilgrimage), especially since the goal of Christian perfection is the love by which we cleave to God. In fact everyone is obligated, to this loving cleaving to God as necessary for salvation, in the form of observing the commandments and conforming to the divine will, and the observation of the commandments excludes everything that is contrary to the nature and habit of love, including mortal sin. Members of religious orders have committed themselves in addition to evangelical perfection, and to the things that constitute a voluntary and counselled perfection by means of which one may arrive more quickly to the supreme goal which is God. The observation of these additional commitments excludes as well the things that hinder the working and fervour of love, and without which one can come to God, and these include the renunciation of all things, of both body and mind, exactly as one's vow of profession entails. Since indeed the Lord God is Spirit, and those who worship him must worship in spirit and in truth, in other words, by knowledge and love, that is, understanding and desire, stripped of all images. This is what is referred to in Matthew 6.6, 'When you pray, enter into your inner chamber,' that is, your inner heart, 'and having closed the door,' that is of your senses, and there with a pure heart and a clear conscience, and with faith unfeigned, 'pray to your Father,' in spirit and in truth, 'in secret.' This can be done best when a man is disengaged and removed from everything else, and completely recollected within himself. There, in the presence of Jesus Christ, with everything, in general and individually, excluded and wiped out, the mind alone turns in security confidently to the Lord its God with its desire. In this way it pours itself forth into him in full sincerity with its whole heart and the yearning of its love, in the most inward part of all its faculties, and is plunged, enlarged, set on fire and dissolved into him.

Cogitavi mihi aliquid ultimate (in quantum possibile est in hujus exsilii et peregrinationis immoratione) depingere, scriptando de et super ab omnibus plena et possibili abstractione, et cum solo Domino Deo expedita, secura, et nuda firmaque adhaesione: praesertim cum ipsius Christianae perfectionis finis sit charitas, qua Domino Deo adhaeretur. Ad quam quidem adhaesionem charitativam omnis homo de necessitate salutis tenetur, quod fit praeceptorum observantia, et divinae voluntatis conformitate: quorum observantia excludit omne quod repugnat charitatis essentiae et habitui, cujusmodi sunt peccata mortalia. Religiosi vero adstrinxerunt se etiam ad Evangelicam perfectionem, atque ad ea quae supererogationis et consilii sunt, per quae expeditius ad ultimum finem, qui Deus est, pervenitur: per quorum observantiam excluduntur ea etiam quae impediunt actum seu fervorem charitatis, quo minus possit quis in Dominum Deum ferri, cujusmodi sunt abrenumtiatio omnium rerum, corporis insuper et animae, professionis dumtaxat voto excepto. Quoniam quidem Spiritus cum sit Dominus Deus, et eos, qui adorant eum, in spiritu et veritate oportet adorare, id est, cognitione et amore, intellectu et affectu, aab omnibus phantasmatibus nudis. Hinc est et illud Matthaei, vi. 6: Cum oraveris, intra in cubiculum tuum, id est, cordis tui intima: et clauso ostio, scilicet sensuum tuorum, et inibi corde puro, et conscientia bona, et fide non ficta, ora Patrem tuum, in spiritu et veritate, in abscondito. Quos tunc congrue fit, cum homo ab omnibus aliis fuerit exoccupatus et exutus, et totus intra se receptus: ubi universis et singulis exclusis et oblitis, coram Jesu Christo, tacito ore, sola mens desideria sua secure Domino Deo suo fiducialiter pandit, ac per hoc toto cordis et amoris affectu se in eum intimissimis medullis omnium virium suarum sincerissime ac plenissime diffundit, et immergit, dilatat et inflammat, et resolvit in se.

How one can cling to and seek Christ alone, disdaining everything else
Qualiter quis, omnibus aliis spretis, soli Christo inhaereat et intendat?

Certainly, anyone who desires and aims to arrive at and remain in such a state must needs above all have eyes and senses closed and not be inwardly involved or worried about anything, nor concerned or occupied with anything, but should completely reject all such things as irrelevant, harmful and dangerous. Then he should withdraw himself totally within himself and not pay any attention to any object entering the mind except Jesus Christ, the wounded one, alone, and so he should turn his attention with care and determination through him into him - that is, though the man into God, through the wounds of his humanity into the inmost reality of his divinity. Here he can commit himself and all that he has, individually and as a whole, promptly, securely and without discussion, to God's unwearying providence, in accordance with the words of Peter, cast all your care upon him (1 Peter 5.7), who can do everything. And again, In nothing be anxious (Philippians 4.6), or what is more, Cast your burden upon the Lord, and he will sustain you. (Psalm 55.22) Or again, It is good for me to hold fast to God, (Ps. 73.28) and I have always set up God before me. (Psalm 16.8) The bride too in the Song of Songs says, I have found him whom my soul loves, (Canticle 3.4) and again, All good things came to me along with her. (Wisdom 7.11) This, after all, is the hidden heavenly treasure, none other than the pearl of great price, which must be sought with resolution, esteeming it in humble faithfulness, eager diligence, and calm silence before all things, and preferring it even above physical comfort, or honour and renown. For what good does it do a religious if he gains the whole world but suffers the loss of his soul? Or what is the benefit of his state of life, the holiness of his profession, the virtue of his habit and tonsure, or the outer circumstances of his way of life if he is without a life of spiritual humility and truth in which Christ abides through a faith created by love. This is what Luke means by, the Kingdom of God (that is, Jesus Christ) is within you. (Luke 17.21)

Verumtamen quicumque talem statum aggredi et ingredi desiderat et satagit, opus est omnino, ut velut clausis oculis et sensibus, de nulla re se penitus implicet aut perturbet, sollicitus sit aut curet: sed cuncta tamquam impertinentia et noxia ac perniciosa funditus excutiat: deinde se totum intra se recipiat, nec aliud umquam objectum inibi mente attendat, quam solum Jesum Christum vulneratum: sicque per eum in eum, id est, per hominem in Deum, per vulnera humanitatis ad intima divinitatis suae, sedulo et obnixe intendat: ibique se suaque singula ac cuncta, indiscusse, suae infatigabili providentiae committat expedite et secure, juxta illud Petri: Omnem sollicitudinem vestram projicientes in eum, qui potest omnia. Et iterum: Nihil solliciti sitis. Et rursus: Jacta super Dominum curam tuam, et ipse te enutriet. Et iterum: Mihi adhaerere Deo bonum est. Et: Providebam Dominum in conspectu meo semper. Et sponsa in Canticis: Inveni quem diligit anima mea: quippe venerunt mihi omnia bona pariter cum illa. Nempe hic est thesaurus ille coelestis absconditus, nec non margarita pretiosa, quae prae omnibus comparata fiducia humili, conatu instantissimo, taciturnitate tranquilla, etiam usque ad corporalis commodi, laudis vel honoris jacturam, in fortitudine spiritus quaeritur. Alioquin quid proficit religiosus, si totum mundum lucretur, et animae suae detrimentum patiatur? Aut quid relevat status, professionis sanctitas, perfectionis habitus, tonsura, et exterioris dispositio conversationis, sine vita in spiritu humilitatis et veritatis, ubi Christus habitat per fidem charitate formatam? Hinc est illud Lucae xvii.21: Regnum Dei intra vos est, quod est Christus Jesus.

What the perfection of man consist of in this life
Quae sit conformitas perfectionis hominis in hac vita?

Now the more the mind is concerned about thinking and dealing with what is merely lower and human, the more it is separated from the experience in the intimacy of devotion of what is higher and heavenly, while the more fervently the memory, desire and intellect is withdrawn from what is below to what is above, the more perfect will be our prayer, and the purer our contemplation, since the two directions of our interest cannot both be perfect at the same time, being as different as light and darkness. He who cleaves to God is indeed translated into the light, while he who clings to the world is in the dark. So the supreme perfection of man in this life is to be so united to God that all his soul with all its faculties and powers are so gathered into the Lord God that he becomes one spirit with him, and remembers nothing except God, is aware of and recognises nothing but God, but with all his desires unified by the joy of love, he rests contentedly in the enjoyment of his Maker alone.

Now the image of God as found in the soul consists of these three faculties, namely reason, memory and will, and so long as they are not completely stamped with God, the soul is not yet deiform in accordance with the initial creation of the soul. For the true pattern of the soul is God, with whom it must be imprinted, like wax with a seal, and carry the mark of his impress. But this can never be complete until the intellect is perfectly illuminated, according to its capacity, with the knowledge of God, who is perfect truth, until the will is perfectly focused on the love of the perfect good, and until the memory is fully absorbed in turning to and enjoying eternal happiness, and in gladly and contentedly resting in it. And since the glory of the beatitude which is achievéd in our heavenly homeland consists in the complete fulfilment of these three faculties, it follows that perfect initiation of them is perfection in this life.

Porro quanto plus mens sollicita est ad ista inferiora et humana cogitanda et tractanda, tanto plus a superioribus et coelestibus per devotionis intima elongatur: et quanto ferventius ab inferiorum memoria, affectu et intellectu ad superiora sensus colligitur, tanto perfectior erit oratio, et purior contemplatio: quia simul perfecte non potest esse utrisque intenta, quae sicut lux et tenebrae sunt divisa. Quippe qui Deo adhaeret, versatur in lumine: qui vero mundo adhaeret, in tenebris est. Qua ex re, est hominis in hac vita sublimior perfectio, ita Deo uniri ut tota anima cum omnibus potentiis suis et viribus in Dominum Deum suum sit collecta, ut unus fiat spiritus cum eo, et nihil meminerit nisi Deum, nihil sentiat vel intelligat nisi Deum, et omnes affectiones in amoris gaudio unitae, in sola Conditoris fruitione suaviter quiescant.

Imago enim Dei in his tribus potentiis in anima expressa consistit, videlicet, ratione, memoria, et voluntate. Et quamdiu illae ex toto, Deo impressae non sunt, non est anima deiformis juxta primariam animae creationem. Forma nempe animae Deus est, cui debet imprimi, sicut cera sigillo, et signatum signo signatur. Hoc autem numquam plene fit, nisi cum ratio perfecte juxta capacitatem suam illuminatur ad cognitionem Dei, qui est summa veritas, et voluntas perfecte afficitur ad amandam summam bonitatem, et memoria plene absorbetur ad intuendum et fruendum aeterna felicitate, et ad suaviter et delectabiliter in ea quiescendum. Et quia in horum consummata adeptione consistit gloria beatudinis, quae perficietur in patria, liquet quod istorum perfecta inchoatio est perfectio in hac vita.

How man's activity should be purely in the intellect and not in the senses

Qualiter operatio humana debeat esse in solo intellectu, et non in sensibus?

Happy therefore is the person who by continual removal of fantasies and images, by turning within, and raising the mind to God, finally manages to dispense with the products of the imagination, and by so doing works within, nakedly and simply, and with a pure understanding and will, on the the simplest of all objects, God. So eliminate from your mind all fantasies, objects, images and shapes of all things other than God, so that, with just naked understanding, intent and will, your practice will be concerned with God himself within you.

For this is the end of all spiritual exercises - to turn the mind to the Lord God and rest in him with a completely pure understanding and a completely devoted will, without the entanglements and fantasies of the imagination. This sort of exercise is not practised by fleshly organs nor by the exterior senses, but by that by which one is indeed a man. For a man is precisely understanding and will. For that reason, in so far as a man is still playing with the products of the imagination and the senses, and holds to them, it is obvious that he has not yet emerged from the motivation and limitations of his animal nature, that is of that which he shares in common with the animals. For these know and feel objects by means of recognised shapes and sense impressions and no more, since they do not possess the higher powers of the soul. But it is different with man, who is created in the image and likeness of God with understanding, will, and free choice, through which he should be directly, purely and nakedly impressed and united with God, and firmly adhere to him.

For this reason the Devil tries eagerly and with all his power to hinder this practice so far as he can, being envious of this in man, since it is a sort of prelude and initiation of eternal life. So he is always trying to draw man's mind away from the Lord God, now by temptations or passions, now by superfluous worries and pointless cares, now by restlessness and distracting conversation and senseless curiosity, now by the study of subtle books, irrelevant discussion, gossip and news, now by hardships, now by opposition, etc. Such matters may seem trivial enough and hardly sinful, but they are a great hindrance to this holy exercise and practice. Therefore, even if they may appear useful and necessary, they should be rejected, whether great or small, as harmful and dangerous, and put out of our minds. Above all therefore it is necessary that things heard, seen, done and said, and other such things, must be received without adding things from the imagination, without mental associations and without emotional involvement, and one should not let past or future associations, implications or constructs of the imagination form and grow.

For when constructs of the imagination are not allowed to enter the memory and mind, a man is not hindered, whether he be engaged in prayer, meditation, or reciting psalms, or in any other practice or spiritual exercise, nor will they recur again.

So commit yourself confidently and without hesitation, all that you are, and everything else, individually and in general, to the unfailing and totally reliable providence of God, in silence and in peace, and he will fight for you.

He will liberate you and comfort you more fully, more effectively and more satisfactorily than if you were to dream about it all the time, day and night, and were to cast around frantically all over the place with the futile and confused thoughts of your mind in bondage, nor will you wear out your mind and body, wasting your time, and stupidly and pointlessly exhausting your strength.

So accept everything, separately and in general, wherever it comes from and whatever its origin, in silence and peace, and with an equal mind, as coming to you from a father's hand and his divine providence. So render your imagination bare of the images of all physical things as is appropriate to your state and profession, so that you can cling to him with a bare and undivided mind, as you have so often and so completely vowed to do, without anything whatever being able to come between your soul and him, so that you can pass purely and unwaveringly from the wounds of his humanity into the light of his divinity.

Felix ergo qui per abstersionem continuam phantasmatum et imaginum, ac per introversionem et inibi per sursum ductionem mentis in Deum, tandem aliquando obliviscitur phantasmatum quodammodo, ac per hoc consequentes operatur interius nudo ac simplici ac puro intellectu et affectu circa objectum simplicissimum Deum. Omnia igitur phantasmata, species, imagines, ac formas rerum omnium citra Deum a mente rejicias, ut in solo nudo intellectu et affectu ac voluntate tuum pendeat exercitium circa Deum intra te.

Nempe finis omnium exercitiorum hic est, scilicet intendere et quiescere in Domino Deo intra te per purissimum intellectum, et devotissimum affectum sine phantasmatibus et implicationibus. Hujusmodi autem exercitium non fit in organis carneis, et sensibus exterioribus, sed per quod quis homo est: homo vero quis est intellectu et affectu. Et idcirco quamdiu homo cum phantasmatibus et sensibus ludit, et eis insistit, videtur nondum exisse motus et limites bestialitatis suae, hoc est, illius quod cum bestiis habet commune. Quia illae per phantasmata et per tales sensitivas seu sensibiles species cognoscunt et afficiuntur, et non aliter, eo quod altiorem vim animae non habeant. Secus est de homine, secundum intellectum et affectum et liberum arbitrium, ad Dei imaginem et similitudinem creato, quibus debet Deo immediate, pure et nude imprimi, et uniri, firmiterque inhaerere.

Quamobrem diabolus diligentissime et maxime conatur impedire illud exercitium, quantum potest, ex quo est quodammodo praeambulum et initium vitae aeternae, invidens super hoc homini. Idcirco nititur semper mentem hominis alienare a Domino Deo, nunc per istas, nunc per illas tentationes seu passiones, nunc sollicitudine superflua et cura indiscreta, nunc turbatione, et conversatione dissoluta, curiositateque irrationabili: nunc per studia librorum subtilium, colloquia aliena, rumores et novitatem: nunc per aspera, nunc per contraria, etc. Quae tamen etsi nonnumquam levia et tamquam nulla videantur peccata, tamen magna sunt impedimenta hujus sancti exercitii et operis. Et ideo, etiamsi utilia et necessaria visa fuerint, sive magna sive parva, ut noxia et perniciosa illico sunt rejicienda penitus, et a sensibus propellenda.

Summopere igitur necessarium est, ut audita, visa, facta, et dicta, et caetera similia sine phantasmatibus, imaginibus et occupationibus recipiantur, nec etiam ex consequenti vel antea vel tunc super hoc phantasmata et implicationes formentur et nutriantur. Et ita quando phantasmata non venit ad memoriam et mentem, tunc non impedit hominem, sive in oratione, meditatione, et psalmodia, sive in alia quacumque operatione et exercitatione spirituali, nec rursum iterato occurret ei.

Et sic expedite secureque te totum, etiam plene omnia et singula committe infallibili et certissimae divinae providentiae cum silentio et quiete, et ipse pugnabit pro te: et melius, honestius ac dulcius liberabit te et consolabitur, quam si tu semper die noctuque de hoc continue phantasiareris, et vana vagaque ac captiva mente fatue sic et sic, hinc et inde discurreres errabundus, necnon mente et corpore deficiens tempus perderes, et vires stulte ac irrationabiliter consumeres.

Cuncta ergo et singula, undecumque et qualitercumque occurrentia ortum habeant, sic accipe cum taciturnitate et tranquillitate acquanimiter, quemadmodum de manu paternae divinaeque providentiae tibi venirent. Nuda igitur te a phantasmatibus omnibus rerum corporearum, juxta tui status et professionis exigentiam, ut nuda mente et sincere inhaereas ei cui te multipliciter et totaliter devovisti, ut nihil quodammodo possibile sit medii inter animam tuam et ipsum, ut pure fixeque fluere possis a vulneribus humanitatis in lumen suae divinitatis.

On purity of heart which is to be sought above all things
De corde puritate, quae est prae omnibus sectanta.

If your desire and aim is to reach the destination of the path and home of true happiness, of grace and glory, by a straight and safe way then earnestly apply your mind to seek constant purity of heart, clarity of mind and calm of the senses. Gather up your heart's desire and fix it continually on the Lord God above. To do so you must withdraw yourself so far as you can from friends and from everyone else, and from the activities that hinder you from such a purpose. Grasp every opportunity when you can find the place, time and means to devote yourself to silence and contemplation, and gathering the secret fruits of silence, so that you can escape the shipwreck of this present age and avoid the restless agitation of the noisy world.

For this reason apply yourself at all times to purity, clarity and peace of heart above all things, so that, so far as possible, you can keep the doors of your heart resolutely barred to the forms and images of the physical senses and worldly imaginations by shutting off the doors of the physical senses and turning within yourself. After all, purity of heart is recognised as the most important thing among all spiritual practices, as its final aim, and the reward for all the labours that a spiritual-minded person and true religious may undertake in this life.

For this reason you should with all care, intelligence and effort free your heart, senses and desires from everything that can hinder their liberty, and above all from everything in the world that could possibly bind and overcome you. So struggle in this way to draw together all the distractions of your heart and desires of your mind into one true, simple and supreme good, to keep them gathered within yourself in one place, and by this means to remain always joined to things divine and to God in your mind, to abandon the unreliable things of earth, and be able to translate your mind continually to the things above within yourself in Jesus Christ.

To which end, if you have begun to strip and purify yourself of images and imaginations and to simplify and still your heart and mind in the Lord God so that you can draw and taste the well of divine grace in everything within yourself, and so that you are united to God in your mind by a good will, then this itself is enough for you in place of all study and reading of holy scripture, and as demonstration of love of God and neighbour, as devotion itself testifies.

So simplify your heart with all care, diligence and effort so that still and at peace from the products of the imagination you can turn round and remain always in the Lord within yourself, as if your mind were already in the now of eternity, that is of the godhead. In this way you will be able to renounce yourself through love of Jesus Christ, with a pure heart, clean conscience and unfeigned faith, and commit yourself completely and fully to God in all difficulties and eventualities, and be willing to submit yourself patiently to his will and good pleasure at all times.

For this to come about you must repeatedly retreat into your heart and remain there, keeping yourself free from everything, so far as is possible. You must always keep the eye of your mind clear and still. You must guard your understanding from daydreams and thoughts of earthly things. You must completely free the inclination of your will from worldly cares and cling with all your being to the supreme true good with fervent love. You must keep your memory always lifted up and firmly anchored in that same true supreme good and only uncreated reality. In just this way your whole mind gathered up with all its powers and faculties in God, may become one spirit with him, in whom the supreme perfection of life is known to consist.

This is the true union of spirit and love by which a man is made compliant to all the impulses of the supreme and eternal will, so that he becomes by grace what God is by nature.

At the same time it should be noted that in the very moment in which one is able, by God's help, to overcome one's own will, that is to cast away from oneself inordinate love or strong feeling, in other words so as to dare simply to trust God completely in all one's needs, by this very fact one becomes so pleasing to God that his grace is imparted to one, and through that very grace one experiences that true love and devotion which drives out all uncertainty and fear and has full confidence in God. What is more, there can be no greater happiness than to place one's all in him who lacks nothing.

So why do you still remain in yourself where you cannot stay. Cast yourself, all of yourself, with confidence into God and he will sustain you, heal you and make you safe. If you dwell on these things faithfully within, they will do more to confer a happy life on you than all riches, pleasures and honours, and above all the wisdom and knowledge of this present deceitful world and its life, even if you were to excel in them all that ever lived.

Si igitur recto et securo tramite ac breviter ad finem beatitudinis viae et patriae, gratiae et gloriae, pervenire desideras et satagis, tunc intenta mente sedulo adspira ad perpetuam cordis munditiam, et puritatem mentis, ac sensuum tranquillitatem: atque cordis affectum recollige, et jugiter defige sursum in Dominum Deum, et inter haec abstrahe te a familiaribus tuis, et ab omnibus hominibus, in quantum in te est, et negotiis hujusmodi propositum tuum impedientibus, semper captans opportunitatem, ubi et quando possis locum, tempus, et modum reperire quietis ac contemplationis, carpens silentii secreta, praesentisque saeculi vitare naufragia, necnon perstrepentis mundi fugere perturbationes.

Qua de re omni tempore puritati, munditiae, ac quieti cordis principaliter stude: ut videlicet continue, velut clausis carnalibus sensibus, in temetipsum convertaris, et cordis ostia a formis et phantasmatibus sensibilium, et imaginationibus terrenorum, quantum possibile est, habeas diligenter serata.

Nempe cordis puritas, inter omnia exercitia spiritualia quodammodo (tamquam finalis intentio, ac laborum omnium retributio, quam in hac vita spiritualis quisque et vere religiosus recipere consuevit) sibi vindicat principatum.

Idcirco cor tuum, sensus, et affectum, cum omni diligentia, solertia et conatu, absolvas ab his omnibus quae libertatem ipsius possent impedire, insuper ab omni re mundi possibilitatem habente alligandi et vincendi te. Sicque cunctas dispersiones cordis, et affectiones mentis, in unum verum, simplex, et principalissimum bonum recolligere, et intra te tamquam in uno loco recollectas habere agoniza, ac per hoc rebus divinis Deoque mente semper inhaerere, atque derelicta fragilitate terrena, cor ad superna in intimis tuis in Jesu Christo jugiter transformare conare.

Quapropter si incipis te nudare et purificare a phantasmatibus et imaginibus, et simplificare et tranquillare fiducialiter in Domino Deo cor tuum et mentem tuam, ut haurias et sentias fontem divini beneplaciti in omnibus interioribus tuis, et per bonam voluntatem sis

Deo unitus in intellectu, sufficit tibi hoc pro omni studio et lectione sacrae Scripturae, et ad dilectionem Dei et proximi, ut unctio docet.

Omni igitur studio, conatu, et labore simplifica cor tuum, ut a phantasmatibus immobilis et tranquillus convertaris, et stes in Domino semper intra te, tamquam si anima tua sit in illo nunc aeternitatis, id est, divinitatis, taliter scilicet, ut amore Jesu Christi, de corde puro, conscientia bona, et fide non ficta teipsum deseras, et totum te Deo in omni tribulatione et eventu totaliter plene committas, ejusque voluntati et beneplacito parere semper et patienter affectes.

Quod ut fiat, necesse est ut frequenter ad cor redeas, et in eo persistas, et ab omnibus, quantum possibile est, teipsum absolvas: mentis oculum semper in puritate et tranquillitate custodias: intellectum a phantasmatibus et formis rerum infirmarum praeserves: voluntatis affectum a curis terrenorum penitus absolvas, et summo vero bono amore fervido radicitus inhaereas: memoriam quoque jugiter habeas sursum elevatum, et in ipso eodem vero summo bono ac solo essentiali et increato firmiter stabilitam: ita dumtaxat, ut tota anima cum omnibus potentiis et viribus suis in Deum recollecta, unus fiat spiritus cum eo, in quo summa perfectio viae consistere cognoscitur.

Haec vero unitas spiritus et amoris est, quo homo omnibus votis supernae et aeternae voluntati conformis efficitur, ut sit per gratiam, quod Deus est per naturam.

Interea animadvertendum, quod in eo ipso momento, quo quis suam Dei auxilio potest vincere voluntatem, id est, inordinatum amorem aut zelum a seipso abjicere, sic scilicet, ut Domino Deo de omni sua necessitate audeat plane totaliter confidere, hoc ipso facto in tantum Deo complacet, ut suam ei gratiam largiatur, et per ipsam gratiam veram sentiat charitatem et dilectionem, omnem ambiguitatem et timorem expellentem, in Deoque confidenter sperantem. Itaque nihil beatius esse potest, quam omnia in illo ponere, in quo nullus est defectus.

Proinde quamdiu stas in te, et non stas, projice te totum in Deum secure, et suscipiet te, sanabit et salvabit te. Haec si continue intra te veraciter revolveris, plus tibi ad beatam vitam conferent, quam omnes divitiae, deliciae, honores, insuper et omnis sapientia et scientia hujus saeculi fallacis, et corruptabilis mundi et vitae, etiamsi in his excelleres omnes qui umquam fuerunt.

That the devout man should cleave to God with naked understanding and will

Quod adhaerere debet homo devotus Deo, nudato intellectu et affectu.

The more you strip yourself of the products of the imagination and involvement in external, worldly things and the objects of the senses, the more your soul will recover its strength and its inner senses so that it can appreciate the things which are above. So learn to withdraw from imaginations and the images of physical things, since what pleases God above everything is a mind bare of those sorts of forms and objects, for it is his delight to be with the sons of men, that is those who, at peace from such activities, distractions and passions, seek him with a pure and simple mind, empty themselves for him, and cleave to him. Otherwise, if your memory, imagination and thought is often involved with such things, you must needs be filled with the thought of new things or memories of old ones, or identified with other changing objects. As a result, the Holy Spirit withholds itself from thoughts bereft of understanding.

So the true lover of Jesus Christ should be so united through good will in his understanding with the divine will and goodness, and be so bare of all imaginations and passions that he does not even notice whether he is being mocked or loved, or something is being done to him. For a good will turns everything to good and is above everything. So if the will is good and is obedient and united to God with pure understanding, he is not hurt even if the flesh and the senses and the outer man is moved to evil, and is slow to good, or even if the inner man is slow to feel devotion, but should simply cleave to God with faith and good will in naked understanding. He is doing this if he is conscious of all his own imperfection and nothingness, recognises his good to consist in his Creator alone, abandons himself with all his faculties and powers, and all creatures, and immerses himself wholly and completely in the Creator, so that he directs all his actions purely and entirely in his Lord God, and seeks nothing apart from him, in whom he recognises all good and all joy of perfection to be found. And he is so transformed in a certain sense into God that he cannot think, understand, love or remember anything but God himself and the things of God. Other creatures however and even himself he does not see, except in God, nor does he love anything except God alone, nor remember anything about them or himself except in God.

This knowledge of the truth always makes the soul humble, ready to judge itself and not others, while on the contrary worldly wisdom makes the soul proud, futile, inflated and puffed up with wind. So let this be the fundamental spiritual doctrine leading to the knowledge of God, his service and familiarity with him, that if you want to truly possess God, you must strip your heart of all love of things of the senses, not just of certain creatures, so that you can turn to the Lord your God with a simple and whole heart and with all your power, freely and without any double-mindedness, care or anxiety, but with full confidence in his providence alone about everything.

Et quia quanto magis te nudaveris a phantasmatibus et implicationibus exterioribus mundanis et sensibilibus, tanto magis anima tua recuperabit vires et interiores sensus suos, ut sapiant ei quae sursum sunt. Disce ergo abstinere a phantasmatibus et imaginibus rerum corporalium, quia super omnia placet Deo mens nuda ab hujusmodi formis et speciebus, cujus etiam deliciae sunt esse cum filiis hominum, videlicet qui a talibus occupationibus et distractionibus et passionibus tranquilla, pura et simplici mente sibi intendunt, vacant et adhaerent. Alioquin si in talibus memoria, imaginatio et cogitatio tua saepe vacat, necesse est, vel rebus novis, vel reliquiis antiquorum deliniri, vel secundum alia objecta varie qualificari. Unde Spiritus sanctus aufert se a cogitationibus quae sunt sine intellectu.

Verus itaque Jesu Christi amator sic debet esse unitus intellectu per bonam voluntatem divinae voluntati et bonitati, et nudus ab omnibus phantasmatibus et passionibus, ut non advertat si derideatur, diligatur, vel quidquid sibi inferatur. Voluntas namque bona omnia complet, super omnia est. Unde si voluntas adsit bona, et Deo in intellectu pure conformis et unita fuerit, non nocet si caro et sensualitas et exterior homo moveatur ad malum, et torpeat ad bonum, aut etiam si interior homo torpet devotionem affectare, sed tantum fide et bona voluntate adhaerere debet Deo in intellectu nude.

Et hoc facit, si omnem imperfectionem et nihileitatem suam animadvertat, et cognoscat bonum suum in solo Creatore consistere, et cum suis potentiis et viribus se ac cunctas creaturas relinquit, atque ex toto et totum se in Creatorem suum immergit, ita quod omnes operationes suas dirigit pure ex toto in Dominum Deum suum, nec extra eum quidquam quaerit, in quo percipit invenisse omne bonum, et omnem felicitatem perfectionis. Et sic transformatur quodammodo in Deum, quod nec cogitare, nec intelligere, nec amare, nec memorare potest, nisi Deum pariter et de Deo: creaturas autem alias et seipsum non videt, nisi tantum in Deo, nec diligit nisi solum Deum, nec memoratur de eis vel de se, nisi in Deo.

Haec vero cognitio veritatis semper facit animam humilem, seipsam, non alium judicantem: sed econtra mundana sapientia facit animam superbam, vanam, turgidam, et vento inflatam. Sit itaque haec spiritualis et fundamentalis doctrina, quod accedens ad Dei notitiam, servitium et familiaritatem, et si vis Deum veraciter possidere, necesse est quod cor tuum denudes omni amore sensibili, non tantum cujuscumque creaturae, ut simplici ac toto corde, secundum omne tuum posse, tendas in Dominum Deum tuum creatorem, libere, absque omni duplicitate, cura et sollicitudine, plena fiducia in sola ejus providentia de omnibus.

How the heart should be gathered within itself
Qualiter cor sit recolligendum intra se?

What is more, as is said in the book On the Spirit and the Soul (of St. Augustine), to ascend to God means to enter into oneself. He who entering within and penetrating his inmost nature, goes beyond himself, he is truly ascending to God. So let us withdraw our hearts from the distractions of this world, and recall them to the inner joys, so that we can establish them to some degree in the light of divine contemplation. For this is the life and peace of our hearts - to be established by intent in the love of God, and to be sweetly remade by his comforting.

But the reason why we are in so many ways hindered in the practical enjoyment of this matter and are unable to get into it is clearly because the human mind is so distracted by worries that it cannot bring its memory to turn within, is so clouded by its imaginations that it cannot return to itself with its understanding, and is so drawn away by its desires that it is quite unable to come back to itself by desire for inner sweetness and spiritual joy. Thus it is so prostrate among the sense objects presented to it that it cannot enter into itself as the image of God.

It is therefore right and necessary for the mind to raise itself above itself and everything created by the abandonment of everything, with humble reverence and great trust, and to say within itself, He whom I seek, love, thirst for and desire from everything and more than anything is not a thing of the senses or the imagination, but is above everything that can be experienced by the senses and the intellect. He cannot be experienced by any of the senses, but is completely desirable to my will. He is moreover not discernable, but is perfectly desirable to my inner affections. He cannot be comprehended, but can be loved in his fullness with a pure heart, for he is above all lovable and desirable, and of infinite goodness and perfection. And then a darkness comes over the mind and it is raised up into itself and penetrates even deeper.

And the more inward-looking the desire for it, the more powerful this means of ascent to the mysterious contemplation of the holy Trinity in Unity and Unity in Trinity in Jesus Christ is, and the more interior the yearning, the more productive it is. Certainly in matters spiritual the more inward they are the greater they are as spiritual experiences.

For this reason, never give up, never stop until you have tasted some pledge, as I might say, or foretaste of the future full experience, and until you have obtained the satisfaction of however small a first fruits of the divine joy. And do not give up pursuing it and following its scent until you have seen the God of gods in Sion. Do not stop or turn back in your spiritual journey and your union and adherence to God within you until you have achieved what you have been seeking.

Take as a pattern of this the example of those climbing an ordinary mountain. If our mind is involved by its desires in the things which are going on below, it is immediately carried away by endless distractions and side tracks, and being to some extent divided against itself, is weakened and as it were scattered amongst the things which it seeks with its desires. The result is ceaseless movement, travel without an arrival, and labour without rest. If on the other hand our heart and mind can withdraw itself by its desire and love from the infinite distraction below of the things beneath it, can learn to be with itself, abandoning these lower things and gathering itself within itself into the one unchanging and satisfying good, and can hold to it inseparably with its will, it is correspondingly more and more gathered together in one and strengthened, as it is raised up by knowledge and desire. In this way it will become accustomed to the true supreme good within itself until it will be made completely immovable and arrive securely at that true life which is the Lord God himself, so that it can now rest in him within and in peace without any changeability or vicissitude of time, perfectly gathered within itself in the secret divine abode in Christ Jesus who is the way for those who come to him, the truth and life.

Praeterea, sicut dicitur in libro de Spiritu et anima, ascendere ad Deum, hoc est intrare in seipsum. Qui enim interius intrans, et intrinsecus penetrans seipsum transcendit, ille veraciter ad Deum ascendit. Ab hujus ergo mundi distractionibus cor nostrum colligamus, et ad interiora gaudia revocemus, ut aliquando in divinae contemplationis lumine hoc figere valeamus. Nam haec est vita et requies cordis nostri, cum in Dei amore per desiderium figitur, et ejus consolatione suaviter reficitur.<

Sed quod in hujus rei experimentali degustatione multipliciter impedimur, et nequaquam ad ipsum pertingere sufficiamus, ratio in promptu est, quia mens humana sollicitudinibus distracta, non intrat se per memoriam, phantasmatibus obumbrata, non redit ad se per intellectum, concupiscentiis illecta, ad seipsam nequaquam revertitur per desiderium suavitatis internae et laetitiae spiritualis: ita totaliter in his sensibilibus et praesentibus jacens, non potest ad se tamquam ad imaginem Dei intrare.

Oportet ergo et necesse est, ut cum humilitatis reverentia ac fiducia nimia mens elevet se supra se et omne creatum per abnegationem omnium, et ut dicat intra se: Quem ex omnibus, et prae omnibus, et super omnia quaero, diligo, appeto, et desidero, non est sensibilis neque imaginabilis, sed super omne sensibile et intelligibile: nullo umquam sensu est perceptibilis, sed pleno desiderio totus desiderabilis: non insuper est figurabilis, sed intimo affectu perfectissime appetibilis: non est aestimabilis, sed mundo corde totus affectibilis, quia super omnia amabilis et delectabilis, infinitaeque bonitatis et perfectionis. Et tunc fertur in mentis caliginem, et altius intra se elevatur, et profundius ingreditur.

Et hic modus ascendendi usque ad aenigmaticum contuitum sanctissimae Trinitatis in unitate, unitatis in Trinitate, in Jesu Christo, tanto est ardentior, quanto vis ascendens illi est intimior: et tanto fructuosior, quanto affectu proximior. Quippe in spiritualibus illa sunt superiora quae intimiora, quoad experientias spirituales.

Quapropter numquam desistas, numquam quiescas, donec futurae illius plenitudinis aliquas (ut ita dicam) arrhas seu experientias degustes, et donec divinae suavitatis dulcedinem per quantulascumque primitias obtineas, et in odorem ipsius post eam currere non desinas, donec videas Deum deorum in Sion. In spirituali enim profectu, et cum Dei intra te unione et adhaesionae, non quiescas, nec retrocedas, donec assecutus fueris quod intendis.

Exemplum hujus accipe in simili ab ascendentibus montem naturalem. Si enim spiritus noster, in his quae deorsum transeunt, se per cupidinem immerserit, statim per infinitas distractiones et itinera obliqua rapitur, et a se quodammodo divisus dissipatur, et quasi in tot spargitur, quot ea sunt quae per desideria concupiscit. Hinc motus sine stabilitate, cursus sine perventione, labor sine requie. Si vero cor et spiritus noster ab hac infimorum infinita distractione, quae deorsum est, per desiderium et amorem se traxerit, et haec infima deferens paulatim se intra se in unum immutabile sufficiens bonum colligens, secum esse didicerit, et ei inseperabiliter quodam affectu inhaeserit, tanto amplius in unum colligitur et fortificatur, quanto magis agnitione et desiderio sursum elevatur, et in ipso vero summo bono intra se habituatur, donec tandem omnino immutabilis fiat, et ad illam veram vitam, quae ipse Dominus Deus est, immutabiliter perveniat: ut perpetuo, sine omni mutabilitatis et temporis vicissitudine, requiescat jam in illo intrinseco, et quieto, ac secreto divinitatis manerio, perfecte collocatus intra se in Christo Jesu, qui est via ad se venientibus, veritas, et vita.

How a religious man should commit himself to God in all circumstances whatsoever

Quomodo in quolibet eventu homo devotus se debeat Deo committere?

I am now completely convinced that you will recognise from these arguments that the more you strip yourself of the products of your imagination and all worldly and created things, and are united to God with your intellect by a good will, the closer you will approach the state of innocence and perfection. What could be better? And what could be more happy and joyful? Above all it is important for you to keep your mind bare - without imaginations and images and free of any sort of entanglement, so that you are not concerned about either the world, friends, prosperity or adversity, or anything present, past or future, whether in yourself or in others - not even your own sins. But consider yourself with a certain pure simplicity to be alone with God outside the world, and as if your mind were already in eternity and separated from the body so that it will certainly not bother about worldly things or be concerned about the state of the world, about peace or war, about good weather or rain, or about anything at all in this world, but with complete docility will turn to God alone, be empty for him and cleave to him. So now in this way ignore your body and all created things, present or future, and direct the high point of your mind and spirit directly, as best you can, naked and unencumbered on the uncreated light. And let your spirit be cleansed in this way from all imaginations, coverings and things obscuring its vision, like an angel (not) tied to a body, who is not hindered by the works of the flesh nor tangled in vain and wandering thoughts.

Let your spirit therefore arm itself against all temptations, vexations, and injuries so that it can persevere steadily in God when attacked by either face of fortune. So that when some inner disturbance or boredom or mental confusion come you will not be indignant or dejected because of it, nor run back to vocal prayers or other forms of consolation, but only to lift yourself up in your intellect by a good will to hold on to God with your mind whether the natural inclination of the body wills it or not. The religious-minded soul should be so united to God and should have or render its will so conformed to the divine will that it is not occupied with any created thing or cling to it any more than before it was created, and as if nothing existed except God and the soul itself. And in this way it should accept everything confidently and equally, in general and in particular, from the hand of divine providence, agreeing in everything with the Lord in patience, peace and silence.

The thing is that the most important thing of all for a spiritual life is to strip the mind of all imaginations so that one can be united in one's intellect to God by a good will, and conformed to him.

Besides, nothing will then be intermediary between you and God. This obvious, since nothing external will stand between you when by the vow of voluntary poverty you will have removed the possession of anything whatsoever, and by the vow of chastity you will have abandoned your body, and by obedience you will have given up your will and your soul itself. And in this way nothing will be left to stand between you and God. That you are a religious person is indicated by your profession, your state, and now your habit and tonsure and such like, but whether you are only a religious in appearance or a real one, you will find out.

Bear in mind therefore how greatly you have fallen away and sin against the Lord your God and all his justice if you behave otherwise and cling with your will and love to what is created rather than to the Creator himself, putting the created before the Creator.

Credo jam et arbitror, quod ex huiusque deductis cognoscas, quod quanto magis magisque te nudaveris a phantasmatibus, et omnibus rebus mundialibus et creatis, ac per bonam voluntatem intellectu Deo unitus fueris, tanto magis ad statum innocentiae et perfectionis appropinquas. Quo quid melius? quidve felicius ac jucundius? Super omnia ergo valet, ut teneas mentem nudam sine phantasmatibus et imaginibus, et a quibuscumque implicationibus, ut nec de mundo, nec de amicis, nec de prosperis, nec de adversis, praesentibus, praeteritis, vel futuris, in te nec in aliis, nec etiam nimis de propriis peccatis solliciteris: sed cum quadam puritatis simplicitate te esse cum Deo extra mundum nude cogita, ac si anima tua jam esset in aeternitate extra corpus separata, utique non tractaret saecularia, nec curaret de statu mundi, nec de pace, nec de guerra nec de sereno, nec de pluvia, et plane nec de aliquo hujus saeculi: sed soli Deo conformiter totaliter intenderet, vacaret, et inhaereret. Sic suo modo vel nunc relinque corpus tuum, et omnia praesentia et futura creata, et defige aciem mentis ac spiritus tui fixe, secundum omne tuum posse, nude et expedite, in illud increatum lumen. Et sic ab omnibus phantasmatibus et involutionibus ac obnubilationibus depuratus sit spiritus tuus, tamquam Angelus corpori alligatus, qui per operationem carnis non impeditur, nec cogitationibus vanis ac vagis implicatur.

Fortificet ergo se spiritus contra quascumque tentationes, vexationes, injurias, ut aequanimiter inconcusse in utraque fortuna perseveret in Deo. Et cum adest turbatio, aut acedia, vel mentis confusio, non propterea insolescas, aut pusillanimis sis, nec propter hoc curras ad orationes vocales, aut alias consolationes: sed hoc solum ut resuscites te per voluntatem bonam in intellectu, ut adhaereas Deo mente, velit nolit sensualitas corporis.

Devota namque anima sic debet esse cum Deo unita, et suam voluntatem divinae voluntati tam conformem habere et facere, quod se cum nulla creatura occupet, seu adhaereat, sicut dum non erat creata: ac si nihil sit praeter solum Deum, et ipsam animam. Et sic universa et singula aequanimiter de manu divinae providentiae secure et infaillibiliter accipiat, sustinens uniformiter in omnibus Dominum in patientia, tranquillitate, et silentio.

Qua de re nudare mentem ab omnibus phantasmatibus super omnia valet ad vitam spiritualem, ut sis per bonam voluntatem unitus Deo in intellectu et conformis.

Praeterea, nihil erit medium inter te et Deum: quod sic patet, quia nec res aliqua ab extra erit medium, cum per votum voluntariae paupertatis ablata sit omnis rei possessio usque ad ultimum, et per castitatis votum corpus, et per obedientiam voluntas et ipsa anima: et sic quodammodo nihil relinquitur, quod mediat inter te et Deum. Quod autem religiosus sis, probat professio ipsa, status tuus, et nunc habitus tuus, et tonsura, et similia hujusmodi: sed an fictus, an verus religiosus sis, tu videris.

Animadverte ergo, quam graviter degeneres et pecces in Dominum Deum tuum, et in omnem ejus justitiam, si secus egeris, et creaturae potius quam Creatori ipsi voluntate et amore inhaeseris, creaturam praeponens Creatori.

How much the contemplation of God is to be preferred to all other exercises

Contemplatio in Deo, quatenus omnibus aliis exercitiis est praeponenda.

Now since all things other than God are the effect and work of the Creator himself, their having ability and being is a limited power and existence, and being as they are created out of nothing, they are circumscribed by the effects of their nothingness, while their tendency of themselves towards nothingness means that we receive our existence, preservation and activity moment by moment from the Creator himself, along with whatever other qualities created things may have, just as we receive their insufficiency to any action of themselves, both with regard to themselves and to others, in relation to him whose operation they are, they remain as a nothing before something which exists, and as something finite before what is infinite. For this reason let all our actual contemplation, life and activity take place in him alone, about him, for him and towards him who is able and capable to produce with a single nod of his will things infinitely more perfect than any that exist now.

No contemplation and fruition of love, whether intellectual or affective, is more useful, more perfect and more satisfying than that which is of God himself, the Creator, our supreme and true Good, from whom, through whom and to whom are all things. He is infinitely satisfying both to himself and to all others, who contains within himself in absolute simplicity and from all eternity the perfection of all things, in whom there is nothing which is not himself, before whom and through whom remain the causes of all things impermanent, and in whom dwell the unchanging origins of all changing things, while even the eternal reasons of all temporal things, rational and irrational, abide in him. He brings everything to completion, and fills all things, in general and in particular, completely and essentially with himself. He is more intimately and more really present to everything by his being than each thing is to itself, for in him all things are united together, and live in him eternally.

What is more, if someone, out of weakness or from lack of intellectual practice, is detained longer in the contemplation of created things, this supreme, true and fruitful contemplation may still be seen as possible for mortal man, so that there may take place an upward leap in all his contemplations and meditations, whether about created things or the Creator, and the appreciation of God the Creator himself, the One and Three, may surge up within so that he come to burn with the fire of divine love and the true life in himself and in others, in such a way as to make him deserving of the joy of eternal life. Even in this one should bear in mind the difference between the contemplation of faithful Catholics and that of pagan philosophers, for the contemplation of the philosophers is for the perfection of the contemplator himself, and consequently it is confined to the intellect and their aim in it is intellectual knowledge. But the contemplation of the Saints, and of Catholics, is for the love of him, that is of the God they are contemplating. As a result it is not confined in the final analysis to the intellect in knowledge, but crosses over into the will through love. That is why the Saints in their contemplation have the love of God as their principal aim, since it is more satisfying to know and possess even the Lord Jesus Christ spiritually through grace than physically or even really but without grace.

Furthermore, while the soul is withdrawn from everything and is turned within, the eye of contemplation is opened and sets itself up a ladder by which it can pass to the contemplation of God. By this contemplation the soul is set on fire for eternal things by the heavenly and divine good things it experiences, and views all the things of time from a distance and as if they were nothing. Hence when we approach God by the way of negation, we first deny him everything that can be experienced by the body, the senses and the imagination, secondly even things experienceable by the intellect, and finally even being itself in so far as it is found in created things. This, so far as the nature of the way is concerned, is the best means of union with God, according to Dionysius. And this is the cloud in which God is said to dwell, which Moses entered, and through this came to the inaccessible light. *Certainly, it is not the spiritual which comes first, but the natural,* (1 Corinthians 15.46) so one must proceed by the usual order of things, from active work to the quiet of contemplation, and from moral virtues to spiritual and contemplative realities. Finally, my soul, why are you uselessly preoccupied with so many things, and always busy with them? Seek out and love the one supreme good, in which is all that is worth seeking, and that will be enough for you. Unhappy therefore is he who knows and possesses everything other than this, and does not know this. While if he knows everything as well as this, it is not from knowing them that he is better off but because of This. That is why John says, *This is eternal life, to know Thee,* etc. (John 17.3) and the prophet says, *I will be satisfied when your glory becomes manifest.* (Psalm 17.15)

Et quia omnia citra Deum sunt effectus et opus ipsius Creatoris, habentia posse et esse, et quidquid sunt et possunt, limitatum, et ut ex nihilo producta nihilitatibus circumdata, et ex se ad nihilum tendentia, necessario momentis singularis suum existere, conservari, operari, et si quid in eis est, et sic per omnia ab ipso summo opifice Deo recipimur, tamquam vere ex seipsis sibi et aliis insufficientia, ad cujus operationem sunt, sicut nihil ad aliquid, finitum ad infinitum. Quapropter in solo eo, et circa eum, et propter eum, et in eum sit omnis recta nostra contemplatio, vita et operatio: qui etiam uno voluntatis nutu posset et sciret in infinitum omnibus modo creatis perfectiora producere.

Nulla ergo, sive secundum intellectum, sive secundum affectum, contemplatio et amoris fruitio utilior, perfectior, et felicior, quam in ipso Deo creatore summo et vero bono, a quo, in quo, per quem, et ad quem omnia: sibi et omnibus sufficiens est in infinitum, qui omnium in se continet perfectiones simplicissime ab aeterno, in quo nihil quod non sit ipse: apud quem, et per quem, omnium instabilium stant causae: in quo omnium mutabilium immutabiles manent origines, necnon omnium rationabilium, irrationabiliumque, atque temporalium in eo sempiternae vivunt rationes: qui omnia complet, universa singulaque se toto essentialiter implet: cuique rei intimior est et praesentialior per essentiam, quam res sibiipsi: in quo omnia simul sunt unita, et in eo sempiterne vivunt.

Praeterea, si ex infirmitate, aut inusitatione intellectus, quis magis tenetur in creaturis contemplari, tunc haec optima, vera, et fructuosa contemplatio videtur homini mortali possibilis, ut saltem in cunctis suis contemplationibus et meditationibus, sive circa creaturas, sive circa Creatorem fiunt, consurgat delectatio in ipso Creatore Deo uno et trino intra se, ut inardescat ignis divini amoris, et verae vitae in se, et in aliis, ut meritum felicitatis aeternae vitae.

Animadvertenda est etiam in hoc differentia inter contemplationem Catholicorum fidelium, et Philosophorum gentilium: quia contemplatio Philosophorum est propter perfectionem contemplantis, et ideo sistit in intellectu, et ita finis eorum in hoc est cognitio intellectus. Sed contemplatio Sanctorum, quae est Catholicorum, est propter amorem ipsius, scilicet contemplati Dei: idcirco non sistit in fine ultimo in intellectu per cognitionem, sed transit ad affectum per amorem. Unde Sancti in contemplatione sua habent amorem Dei tamquam principaliter intentum, quia felicius est etiam Dominum Jesum Christum cognoscere, et habere spiritualiter per gratiam, quam sine gratia corporaliter, vel etiam essentialiter.

Porro dum anima ab omnibus abstrahitur, et in seipsam reflectitur, contemplationis oculus dilatatur, et se scalam erigit, per quam transeat ad contemplandum Deum. Ex qua contemplatione anima inardescit ab bona coelestia et divina, et ad aeterna, et omnia temporalia a longe prospicit tamquam nihil sint. Unde quando in Deum procedimus per viam remotionis, primo negamus ab eo omnia corporalia et sensibilia et imaginabilia, secundo etiam intelligibilia, ad ultimum, hoc ipsum esse secundum quod in creaturis remanet. Sic quantum ad statum viae pertinet, optime Deo conjungimur, secundum Dionysium. Et haec caligo est, quam Deus inhabitare dicitur, quam Moyses intravit, ac per hanc ad lucem inaccessibilem. Verum *non prius quod spiritale est, sed quod animale*: ideo consueto ordine procedendum est a labore actionis ad quietum contemplationis, a virtutibus moralibus ad theoricas et speculativas.

Denique, o anima mea, quid occuparis circa plurima supervacue, et semper in his eges? Intende et ama hoc unum optimum bonum, in quo omne bonum, et sufficit. Infelix ergo qui omnia scit praeter ipsum et habet, ipsum autem nescit. Et si haec omnia et ipsum sciat, non propter hoc, sed propter ipsum beatior. Unde, Joannis, xvii,3: *Haec est vita aeterna: ut cognoscant te*, etc. Et Propheta: *Satiabor cum apparuerit gloria tua.*

That one should not be concerned about feeling tangible devotion so much as about cleaving to God with one's will
Actualis devotio et sensibilis non tantum curanda est, sicut voluntate Deo adhaerere.

Furthermore you should not be much concerned about tangible devotion, the experience of sweetness or tears, but rather that you should be mentally united with God within yourself by a good will in your intellect. For what pleases God above everything is a mind free from imaginations, that is images, ideas and the representations of created things. It befits a monk to be indifferent to everything created so that he can turn easily and barely to God alone within himself, be empty for him and cleave to him.

For this reason deny yourself so that you can follow Christ, the Lord your God, in nakedness, who was himself poor, obedient, chaste, humble and suffering, and in whose life and death many were scandalised, as is clear from the Gospel accounts.

After all, a soul which is separated from the body pays no attention to what is done to its abandoned body - whether it is burned, hanged, or reviled, and is in no way saddened by the afflictions imposed on the body, but thinks only of the Now of eternity and the One Thing which the Lord calls necessary in the Gospel. So you too should treat your body as if you were no longer in the body, but think always of the eternity of your soul in God, and direct your thoughts carefully to that One Thing of which Christ said, For one thing is necessary. (Luke 10.42) You will experience because of it great grace, helping you towards the acquisition of nakedness of mind and simplicity of heart. Indeed this One Thing is very much present with you if you have made yourself bare of imaginations and all other entanglements, and you will soon experience that this is so - namely when you can be empty and cleave to God with a naked and resolute mind. In this way you will remain unconquered in whatever may be inflicted on you, like the holy martyrs, fathers, the elect, and indeed all the saints who despised everything and only thought of their souls' security and eternity in God. Armed in this way within, and united to God through a good will, they spurned everything of the world as if their souls were already separated from their bodies.

Consider from this how much a good will united with God is capable of, when by means of its pressing towards God the soul is effectively separated the body in spirit and looks on its outward man as it were from a distance, and as not belonging to it. In this way it despises everything that is inflicted on itself or on its flesh as if they were happening to someone else, or not to a human being at all. For He that is united with the Lord is one Spirit, (1 Corinthians 6.17) that is with him. So you should never dare to think or imagine anything before the Lord your God that you would blush to be heard or seen in before men, since your respect for God should be even greater than for them.

It is a matter of justice in fact that all your thoughts and thinking should be raised to God alone, and the highest point of your mind should only be directed to him as if nothing existed but him, and holding to him may enjoy the perfect beginning of the life to come.

Praeterea, non multum cures actualem devotionem, aut sensibilem dulcedinem, vel lacrymas, sed tantum per bonam voluntatem in intellectu sis mente cum Deo intra te unitus. Quippe super omnia placet Deo mens nuda a phantasmatibus, id est, imaginibus, speciebus, ac similitudinibus rerum creatarum. Decet namque monachum esse alienum ab omni creatura, ut soli Deo intra se nude et expedite intendat, vacet, et adhaereat.

Quamobrem abneges temetipsum, ut nude sequaris Christum Dominum Deum tuum, qui vere pauper, obediens, castus, humiliatus est, et passus: in cujus etiam vita et morte multi scandalizati fuerunt, ut liquet ex decursu Evangelii.

Praeterea, anima separata a corpore non advertit quomodo aut quid agatur de suo corpore derelicto, sive comburatur, sive suspendatur, sive maledicatur, et nihil propter has injurias corpori illatas contristatur, sed solum cogitat illud nunc aeternitatis, et illud unum quod dicit Dominus in Evangelio necessarium. Sic et tu te habeas ad corpus tuum, quasi jam non sis in corpore, et cogita semper de aeternitate animae tuae in Deo, et dirige sedulo cogitatum tuum in illud unum de quo Christus dixit: Porro unum est necessarium: et senties ex hoc magnam gratiam, ad mentis nuditatem et cordis simplificationem acquirendam.

Verumtamen istud unum est tibi praesentissimum, si te nudaveris a phantasmatibus, et quibuscumque aliis implicationibus, moxque senties sic esse, videlicet te nuda et expedita mente vacare et adhaerere Deo: et sic eris invictus etiam in omnibus qualitercumque inferri possunt, sicut et sancti Martyres, Patres et electi, beatique omnes: qui, despectis omnibus, solum cogitabant animae securitatem et aeternitatem in Deo: et ita armati intus, et per bonam voluntatem Deo uniti, omnia mundi spreverunt, ac si omnino anima jam divisa esset a corpore.

Ex his ergo perpende, quantum potest bona voluntas cum Deo unita, imo per illam animae impressionem in Deo, ut per ejus a carne virtualem et spiritualem divisionem, anima quodammodo respiciat a longe hominem exteriorem suum tamquam non suum; et sic vilipendit omnia quae inferuntur sibi vel carni suae, ac si fierent alteri, vel non homini. *Qui* enim *adhaeret Domino, unus spiritus est,* scilicet cum eo. Numquam ergo audeas omnino coram Domino Deo tuo intra te aliquid cogitare, vel imaginari, quod coram hominibus erubesceres vel audiri, vel videri, propter Dei reverentiam principalem.

Est etiam hoc justum, omnem tuum cogitatum et cogitationem ad solum Deum erigere: eumque, tamquam nihil aliud praeter ipsum sit, sola mentis acie intueri, sicque inhaerendo frui, quod est perfecta inchoatio vitae futurae.

How one should resist temptations and bear trials
Qualiter tentationibus sit resistendum, et tribulationes qualiter sustinendae?

Now there is no one who approaches God with a true and upright heart who is not tested by hardships and temptations.

So in all these temptations see to it that even if you feel them, you do not consent to them, but bear them patiently and calmly with humility and long suffering. Even if they are blasphemies and sordid, hold firmly on to this fact in everything, that you can do nothing better or more effective against them than to consider all this sort of fantasy as a nothing. Even if they are the most vile, sordid and horrible blasphemies, simply take no notice of them, count them as nothing and despise them. Don't look on them as yours or allow yourself to make them a matter of conscience. The enemy will certainly take flight if you treat him and his company with contempt in this way. He is very proud and cannot bear to be despised and spurned. So the best remedy is to completely ignore all such temptations, like flies flying around in front of your eyes against your will.

The servant of Jesus Christ must see to it that he is not so easily forced to withdraw from the face of the Lord and to be annoyed, murmur and complain over the nuisance of a single fly, that is, a trivial temptation, suspicion, sadness, distraction, need or any such adversity, when they can all be put to flight with no more than the hand of a good will directed up to God. After all, through a good will a man has God as his defender, and the holy angels as his guardians and protectors. What is more, any temptation can be overcome by a good will too, like a fly driven away from a bald head by one's hand.

So peace is for men of good will. Indeed we can offer God nothing more valuable than a good will, since a good will in the soul is the source of all good things, and the mother of all virtues. If any one is beginning to possess that good will, he undoubtedly has what is necessary for leading a good life. For if you want what is good, but cannot do it, God will make good the deed.

For it is in accordance with this eternal law that God has established with irrevocable firmness that deserts should be a matter of the will, whether in bliss or torment, reward or punishment. Love itself is a great will to serve God, a sweet desire to please God, and a fervent wish to experience God. What is more, to be tempted is not a sin, but the opportunity for exercising virtue, so that temptation can be greatly to a man's benefit, since it is held that the whole of a man's life on earth is a testing. (Job 7.1)

Proinde nemo accedens ad Deum vero et integro corde est, quin vexationibus et tentationibus probetur.

Idcirco in omnibus tentationibus vel hoc observetur, ut si sentiatur, non consentiatur, et patienter ac aequanimiter cum humilitate et longanimitate portetur. Si vero blasphemiae sint et turpissimae, hoc omnino firmiter teneas, quod nihil melius aut verius contra easdem facere potes, quam omnino hujusmodi phantasias pro nihilo reputare: quamquam blasphemiae nequissimae et foedissimae et horribiles sint, solum non cura eas, sed pro nihilo reputa et contemne, et tibi non imputa, nec velis tibi super hujusmodi conscientiam formare. Fugiet procul dubio inimicus, si eum sic et suas factiones contempseris. Superbus enim est valde, non patitur se contemni et sperni. Omnino ergo talia penitus non curare, summum est remedium, sicut de muscis volantibus coram oculis contra voluntatem.

Provideat ergo servus Jesu Christi, tam facile non importune fugere a facie Domini, et hinc inde indignari, murmurare, et querulari super unius muscae vexatione, videlicet levis tentationis, suspicionis, tristitiae, et detractionis, insufficientiae, et cujuscumque adversitatis, cum sola manu bonae voluntatis in Deum erectae possunt omnia haec fugari. Nempe per bonam voluntatem habet homo Deum in defensorem, sanctos Angelos custodes et protectores. Insuper et per bonam voluntatem omnis tentatio superatur, sicut musca manu de calvitie capitis fugatur.

Pax ergo *hominibus bonae voluntatis.* Proinde ergo nec aliquid ditius offertur Deo bona voluntate. Quippe bona voluntas in anima, est origo omnium bonorum, et omnium mater virtutum: quam qui habere incipit, secure habet quidquid ei ad bene vivendum opus est. Si ergo volueris bonum, et non potes, factum Deus compensat.

Igitur secundum hoc aeterna lex incommutalibili stabilitate firmavit, ut in voluntate meritum sit: in beatitudine aut in miseria, praemium atque supplicium. Dilectio enim est magna voluntas Deo serviendi, dulcis affectus Deo placendi, ferventissimum desiderium Deo fruendi. Demum, tentari non est peccatum, sed materia exercendae virtutis, ut homo ad multa bona proficiat tentatione, cum tota vita hominis super terram tentatio censeatur.

How powerful the love of God is
De amore Dei, quam efficax sit.

All that is said above and whatever is necessary for salvation cannot be better, more immediately and more securely achieved than by love, through which whatever is lacking of what is necessary for salvation can be made good. In love we possess the fullness of all good and the realisation of our highest longing is not denied us. After all it is love alone by which we turn back to God, are changed into God, cleave to God, and are united to God in such a way that we become one spirit with him, and are by him and through him made blessed here by grace and hereafter in glory. Now love is such that it cannot rest except in the beloved, but it does when it wins the beloved in full and peaceful possession. For love, which itself is charity, is the way of God to men and the way of man to God. God cannot house where there is no love. So if we have love, we have God, for God is love. Furthermore nothing is sharper than love, nothing is more subtle, nothing more penetrating. It will not rest until it has by its very nature penetrated the whole power, the depth and the totality of the loved one. It wants to make itself one with the beloved, and itself, if it were possible, to be what the beloved is too. Thus it cannot bear that anything should stand between itself and the beloved object, which is God, but presses eagerly towards him. As a result it never rests until it has left everything else behind and come to him alone.

For the nature of love is of a unitive and transforming power which transforms the lover into what he loves, or alternatively, makes the lover one with the other, and vice versa, in so far as is possible. This is manifest in the first place with regard to the mental powers, depending on how much the beloved is in the lover, in other words depending on how sweetly and delightfully the beloved is recalled in the mind of the lover, and in direct proportion, that is, with how much the lover strives to grasp all the things that relate to the beloved not just superficially but intimately, and to enter, as it were, into his innermost secrets. It is also manifest with regard to the emotional and affective powers when the beloved is said to be in the lover, in other words when the desire to please the beloved is found in the will and established within by the happy enjoyment of him. Alternatively, the lover is in the beloved when he is united with him by all his desire and compliance in agreement with the beloved's willing and not willing, and finds his own pleasure and pain in that of the beloved. For love draws the lover out of himself (since love is strong as death), and establishes him in the beloved, causing him to cleave closely to him. For the soul is more where it loves than where it lives, since it is in what it loves in accordance with its very nature, understanding and will, while it is in where it lives only with regard to form, which is even true for animals as well.

There is nothing therefore which draws us away from the exterior senses to within ourselves, and from there to Jesus Christ and things divine, more than the love of Christ and the desire for the sweetness of Christ, for the experience, awareness and enjoyment of the presence of Christ's divinity. For there is nothing but the power of love which can lead the soul from the things of earth to the lofty summit of heaven. Nor can anyone attain the supreme beatitude unless summoned to it by love and yearning. Love after all is the life of the soul, the wedding garment and the soul's perfection, containing all the law and the prophets and our Lord's teaching. That is why Paul says to the Romans, Love is the fulfilling of the law, (Rom. 13.8) and in the first letter to Timothy, The end of the commandment is love. (1 Timothy 1.5)

Enimvero omnia supradicta, et quaecumque saluti necessaria, non melius, nec propinquius, nec salubrius perfici possunt, nisi per amorem: per quem suppleri potest omnis necessarii ad salutem indigentia, et in eo habetur omnis boni abundantia, nec deest summi desiderii praesentia. Quippe solus amor est, quo convertimur ad Deum, transformamur in Deum, adhaeremus Deo, unimur Deo, ut simus unus spiritus cum eo, et beatificemur hic in gratia, et ibi in gloria, ab eo, et per eum. Amor enim ipse non quiescit, nisi in amato, quod fit cum obtinet ipsum possessione plenaria atque pacifica. Nempe amor ipse, qui et charitas, est via Dei ad homines, et via hominis ad Deum: et mansionem Deus habere non potest, ubi charitas non est. Si igitur charitatem habemus, Deum habemus, quia *Deus charitas est*. Proinde nihil amore acutius, nihil subtilius aut penetrabilius: nec quiescit, donec naturaliter totam amabilis penetraverit virtutem et profunditatem ac totalitatem, et unum se vult facere cum amato, et si fieri potest, ut hoc idem ipse sit quod amatum. Et ita nullum patitur mediam inter se et objectum dilectum quod amat, quod est Deus, sed vehementer tendit in eum: et ideo numquam quiescit, donec omnia transeat, et ad ipsum in ipsum veniat.

Est enim amor ipse virtutis unitivae et transformativae, transformans amantem in amatum, et econtra, ut sit unum amatorum in altero, et e converso, in quantum intimius potest. Quod liquet primo quantum ad vires apprehensivas, qualiter amatum sit in amante: videlicet in quantum dulciter et delectabiliter revocatur in apprehensione amantis: et e regione, prout scilicet amans nititur singula quae ad amatum pertinent, non superficialiter, sed intrinsecus discernere, et quasi ad interiora ejus ingredi. Sed quantum ad vires appetitivas et affectivas, amatum dicitur in amante, prout videlicet est in affectuosa ejus complacentia, et in jucunda ejus delectatione interius radicata: e converso, amans est in amato, toto desiderio et conformitate secundum idem velle et nolle, et in eodem gaudere et tristari, tamquam idem ipse. Trahit enim amor (quia *fortis est ut mors dilectio*) amantem extra se, et collocat eum in amato, faciens ei intimissime inhaerere. Plus enim est anima ubi amat, quam ubi animat: quia sic est in amato secundum propriam naturam, rationem, et voluntatem: sed in eo quod animat, tantum est secundum quod est forma: quod etiam brutis convenit.

Non est ergo aliud quod nos ab exterioribus sensibilibus intra nos, et exinde in Jesu Christi intima et divina trahit, quam amor Christi, quam desiderium dulcedinis Christi, ad sentiendum, percipiendum, et degustandum praesentiam divinitatis Christi. Non itaque aliud est quam amoris vis, quae etiam animam de terris ad fastigia coeli celsa perducit. Nec ad summam beatitudinem quis pervenire potest, nisi amore et desiderio provocante. Ipse etiam amor est vita animae, vestis nuptialis, et perfectio ipsius, in quo omnis lex et Prophetae, et Domini edictum pendet. Under Apostolus ad Romanos: *Plenitudo legis est dilectio.* Et prima ad Timotheum: *Finis praecepti est charitas.*

The nature and value of prayer, and how the heart should be recollected within itself

Orationis qualitas et utilitas: quomodo cor sit recolligendum intra se?

Besides this, since we are incapable of ourselves for this and for any other good action whatsoever, and since we can of ourselves offer nothing to the Lord God (from whom all good things come) which is not his already, with this one exception, as he has deigned to show us both by his own blessed mouth as well as by his example, that we should turn to him in all circumstances and occasions as guilty, wretched, poor, beggarly, weak, helpless, subject servants and sons. And that we should beseech him and lay before him with complete confidence the dangers that are besetting us on all sides, completely grief-stricken in ourselves, in humble prostration of mind, in fear and love, and with recollected, composed, mature, true and naked, shamefaced affection, with great yearning and determination, and in groaning of heart and sincerity of mind. Thus we commit and offer ourselves up to him freely, securely and nakedly, fully and in everything that is ours, holding nothing back to ourselves, in such a complete and final way, that the same is fulfilled in us as in our blessed father Isaac, who speaks of this very type of prayer, saying, Then we shall be one in God, and the Lord God will be all in all and alone in us when his own perfect love, with which he first loved us, will have become the disposition of our own hearts too. This will come about when all our love, all our desire, all our concern, all our efforts, in fact everything we think, everything we see, speak and even hope will be God, and that unity which now is of the Father with the Son, and of the Son with the Father, will be poured into our own heart and mind as well, in such a way that just as he loves us with sincere and indissoluble love we too will be joined to him with eternal and inseparable affection. In other words we shall be united with him in such a way that whatever we hope, and whatever we say or pray will be God.

This therefore should be the aim, this the concern and goal of a spiritual man - to be worthy to possess the image of future bliss in this corruptible body, and in a certain measure experience in advance how the foretaste of that heavenly bliss, eternal life and glory begins in this world. This, as I say, is the goal of all perfection, that his purified mind should be daily raised up from all bodily objects to spiritual things until all his mental activity and all his heart's desire become one unbroken prayer. So the mind must abandon the dregs of earth and press on towards to God, on whom alone should be fixed the desire of a spiritual man, for whom the least separation from that summum bonum is to be considered a living death and dreadful loss. Then, when the requisite peace has been established in his mind, when it is free from attachment to any carnal passion, and clings firmly in intention to that one supreme good, the Apostle's sayings are fulfilled, Pray without ceasing, (1 Thessalonians 5.17) and, Pray in every place lifting up pure hands without anger or dispute. (1 Timothy 2.8) For when the power of the mind is absorbed in this purity, so to speak, and is transformed from an earthly nature into the spiritual or angelic likeness, whatever it receives into itself, whatever it is occupied with, whatever it is doing, it will be pure and sincere prayer.

In this way, if you continue all the time in the way we have described from the beginning, it will become as easy and clear for you to remain in contemplation in your inward and recollected state, as to live in the natural state.

Praeterea, cum ad haec et ad quaecumque alia bona omnino simus ex nobis insufficientes, nec aliquid de nobis ipsi Domino Deo (a quo solo omne bonum) exhibere possumus, quod non sit prius suum, solo uno excepto, quod superest, quemadmodum ipse per se benedicto suo ore etiam et exemplo nos instruere dignatus est, ut videlicet in omni casu et eventu ad ipsam orationem recurramus, sicut rei, miseri, pauperes, mendici, infirmi, inopes, subditi, servi, et filii, ac totaliter in nobis ipsis desolati, humiliata mentis prostratione, in timore et amore, recollecte et composite, maturo, vero, nudoque affectu erubescentiae cum magnitudine desiderii et ardore, necnon in gemitu cordis, et simplicitate et sinceritate mentis, supplicemus et exponamus ipsi plena cum fiducia undique nobis imminentia pericula; ita dumtaxat, ut expedite, secure, et nude nos ei totaliter usque ad ultimum videlicet committamus, et offeramus, tamquam vere et per omnia sui, nihil nobisipsis reservantes, ut impleatur in nobis illud beati patris Isaac, qui loquitur de hac ipsa oratione, dicens: 'Tunc erimus unum in Deo, et Dominus Deus erit in nobis omnia in omnibus et solus, quando illa sua perfecta dilectio, qua prior ille nos dilexit, in nostri quoque cordis transierit affectum.' Quod ita fiet, cum nobis omnis amor, omne desiderium, omne studium, omnis conatus, denique omnis cogitatio nostra, omneque quod videmus, loquimur, quodque speramus, Deus erit, illaque unitas quae nunc est Patris cum Filio, et Filii cum Patre, in nostrum fuerit sensum mentemque transfusa: ut quemadmodum ille nos sincera et pura atque indissolubili charitate diligit, nos quoque ei perpetua et inseparabili dilectione jungamur: ita scilicet eidem copulati, ut quidquid speramus, quidquid intelligimus, quidquid loquimur et oramus, Deus sit.

Haec ergo intentio, hic conatus, et finis spiritualis hominis esse debet, ut imaginem futurae beatitudinis in hoc corruptibili corpore possidere mereatur, et quodammodo arrham illius coelestis beatitudinis et conversationis et gloriae incipiat in hoc saeculo praegustare. Hic, inquam, finis totius perfectionis est, ut eo usque extenuata mens ab omni situ carnali, ad spiritualia quotidie sublimetur, donec omnis conversatio, omnisque voluntas cordis, una et jugis efficiatur oratio. Cumque ita mens, deposita faece terrena, ad Deum, in quo solo semper defixa debet esse intentio spiritualis hominis, respiraverit (cui ab illo summo bono vel parva separatio, mors praesens ac perniciosissimus interitus est credendus) praemissaque fuerit tranquillitate fundata, vel ab omnium carnalium passionum nexibus absoluta, et illi uni summoque bono tenacissima adhaesit intentione, Apostolicum illud implebit: *Sine intermissione orate*. Et: *Orate in omni loco, levantes puras manus, sine ira et disceptatione*. Haec enim puritate (si dici potest) sensu mentis absorpto, ac de terreno situ ad spiritualem sive angelicam similitudinem transformato, quidquid in se receperit, quidquid tractaverit, quidquid egerit, purissima atque sincerissima oratio erit.

Haec proinde si continuaveris indisrupte, quemadmodum usque ab initio disseruimus, erit tibi in tua introversione et recollectione jam facile ac promptum contemplari ac frui, sicut vivere in natura.

That we should seek the verdict of our conscience in every decision
Conscientiae attestatio in omni judicio requirenda est.

While we should strive for spiritual perfection of mind, purity and peace in God, it will be found to be not a little beneficial to this that we should return quietly into the inner secret place of the mind in the face of everything said, thought or done to us. There, withdrawn from everything else and completely recollected within ourselves, we can place ourselves in the knowledge of the truth before us and undoubtedly discover and understand that it does us absolutely no good, and rather the contrary, when we are praised or honoured by others while we recognise by the knowledge of the truth about ourselves within that we are blameworthy and guilty. And just as nothing is any help if externally people praise someone if his conscience internally accuses him, in the same way on the contrary it does a man no harm to be despised, maligned and persecuted when he remains internally just as innocent, blameless and without fault. On the contrary he has all the more good reason to rejoice in the Lord with patience, in peace and silence. After all no adversity can do any harm where evil is not in control, and just as no evil goes unpunished, so no good goes unrewarded. Nor should we wish a reward with hypocrites or expect and receive profit from men, but from the Lord God alone, not in the present, but in the future, and not in fleeting time, but in eternity.

It is clear therefore that nothing is greater, and nothing better than to enter into the inner secret place of the mind always and in every tribulation and occurrence, and there to call upon the Lord Jesus Christ himself, our helper in temptations and tribulations, and to humble ourselves there by confession of sin, and praise God and Father himself, the giver of correction and the giver of consolation. Above all one should accept everything, in general and individually, in oneself or in others, agreeable or disagreeable, with a prompt and confident spirit, as coming from the hand of his infallible Providence or the order he has arranged.

This attitude will lead to the forgiveness of our sins, the deliverance from bitterness, the enjoyment of joy and security, the outpouring of grace and mercy, introduction and establishment into a close relationship with God, abundant enjoyment of his presence, and firm cleaving and union with him. But let us not copy those who from hypocrisy and Pharisaism want to appear better and different from what they are, and to make a better impression and appearance before men of being something special, than they know in truth inside to be so. For it is absolute madness to seek, hunger for and aspire to human praise or renown, from oneself or others, when one is in spite of it all inwardly full of cravings and serious faults. And certainly the good things we have talked about above will flee him who chases such vanities, and he will merely bring disgrace on himself.

So always keep your faults and your own incapacity before your eyes, and know yourself, so that you can be humbled and not try to avoid being held as the lowest, vilest and most abject scum by everyone when you are aware of the grave sins and serious faults in yourself. For which reason consider yourself compared to others as dross to gold, weeds to the wheat, chaff to the grain, a wolf to the sheep, Satan to the children of God. And do not seek to be respected by others and given precedence before others, but rather flee with all your heart and soul the poison of this disease, the venom of praise, the concern for boasting and vanity, lest, as the prophet says, The wicked is praised in his own heart's desires, (Psalm 10.4) and Isaiah, They who speak good of you, deceive you and destroy the way of your feet, (Isaiah 3.12) and the Lord in Luke, Woe to you when men speak well of you! (Luke 6.26).

Demum ad spiritualem mentis perfectionem, puritatem, et tranquillitatem in Deo consequendam, non mediocriter ad hoc proficere videtur, ut in omni quod de nobis dicitur, sentitur, et agitur, semper tacite ad interiora mentis arcana recurramus, et inibi ab omnibus alio abstracti, et intra nos totaliter recollecti, statuamus nos in cognitionem veritatis ante nos, et utique inveniemus atque videbimus penitus nihil proficere nobis, sed plurimum obesse, si laudati vel honorati ab extra fuerimus, et ab intra in veritatis cognitione de nobis culpabiles et rei existimus. Et sicut tunc nihil prodest, si quempiam ab extra homines laudant, et conscientia ab intra accusat: ita e regione nihil obest, si ab extra quis contemptus, vituperatus, et persecutus fuerit, ab intra tantum innocens, irreprehensibilis, et innoxius existat: imo quam plurimum super haec cum patientia, et silentio, et quiete, non immerito in Domino gratulari habet: siquidem nulla nocebit adversitas, ubi non dominatur iniquitas. Et sicut nullum malum impunitum, ita nullum bonum irremuneratum. Neque cum hypocritis velimus mercedem et praemium exspectare, vel recipere ab hominibus: sed solum a Domino Deo, non in praesenti, sed in futuro, non transitorio in tempore, sed in aeternitate.

Liquet ergo, quod nec majus aliquid, nec melius, quam semper in omni tribulatione et eventu ire ad interiora mentis secreta, et ibi invocare ipsum Dominum Jesum Christum, adjutorem in tentationibus et tribulationibus, ac inibi humiliari in confessione peccati, laudare ipsum Deum et Patrem, corripientem et consolantem: insuper et omnia et singula, in se vel in aliis, prospera sive adversa, aequanimiter accipere, expedite et secure, de manu suae infalltbilis providentiae aut dispositionis ordinate.

Ex quibus sequitur etiam peccatorum remissio, amaritudinis expressio, collatio dulcedinis et securitatis, unfusio gratiae et misericordiae, attractio et corroboratio familiaritatis, atque abundans in ipso consolatio, firmaque adhaesio et unio. Sed nec velimus imitari eos, qui per hypocrisim, et more Pharisaico, seipsos carius et aliter videri, haberi et apparere ab extra coram hominibus satagunt, quam ab intra in veritate de se didicerunt: quod quidem extremae dementiae est, sic videlicet quaerere, appetere aut expetere laudem humanam vel gloriam a se vel ab aliis, cum nihilominus interius repletus sit illecebris et peccatis gravissimis. Et certe qui post hujusmodi vanissima currit, fugient ab eo praedicta bona, et dedecus incurret.

Semper ergo prae oculis tuis habeas mala tua, et inidoneitatem tuam, et cognosce te, ut humilieris, et tamquam peripsema indignissimum, vilissimum, abjectissimumque ab omnibus haberi non refugias propter gravissima peccata et maxima mala tua. Qua de re reputa te inter alios, ut scoriam inter aurum, zizaniam inter triticum, paleam inter grana, lupum inter oves, satan inter filios Dei. Sed nec velis revereri ab aliis, aliisque praeferri: imo potius toto corde et spiritu fuge virus hujus pestilentiae, venenum laudis, reputationem jactantiae et ostentationis, ne videlicet, juxta Prophetam, *laudetur peccator in desideriis animae suae*. Et, Isaiae, iii.12: *Qui beatum te dicunt, ipsi te decipiunt, et viam gressuum tuorum dissipant*. Et Dominus, Lucae, vi.26: *Vae cum benedixerint vobis homines*.

How contempt of himself can be produced in a man, and how useful it is

Contemptus sui, qualiter causetur in homine, et quam utilis sit?

Furthermore the more a man recognises his own insignificance, the more he fully and the more clearly he becomes aware to the divine majesty, and the more a man is low in his own eyes for the sake of God, the truth and justice, the more precious he is in the eyes of God.

For this reason let us strive with the whole strength of our desire to consider ourselves the lowest of all and to consider ourselves unworthy of any favour. We should strive to be displeasing to ourselves and pleasing only to God, while regarded as low and unworthy of consideration by others. Above all not to be moved by difficulties, afflictions and insults, and not to be upset by those who inflict such things on us, or entertain evil thoughts against them or be indignant, but to believe steadfastly and with equanimity in all insults, slights, blows and dereliction that it is only appropriate. For in truth he who is really penitent and grieving before God hates to be honoured and loved by all, and does not try to manipulate things so as to avoid being to some degree hated, neglected and despised right to the end, so that he can be truly humbled and sincerely cleave to God alone with a pure heart.

Indeed, for loving God alone and hating oneself more than anything, and desiring to be despised by others we do not require external work or physical strength, but rather physical solitude, the labour of the heart, and peace of mind so that, as it were, by labour of the heart and the disposition of the inmost mind, one may rise up, casting off from oneself lower and physical things, and so soar up, ascending to things heavenly and divine.

For indeed in so doing we changed into God, and this will especially take place when without judgement, condemnation or contempt of our neighbour, we choose rather to be considered as scum and a disgrace by everyone and to be despised as unclean filth by everyone than to experience all sorts of different delicacies or to be honoured and exalted by men, or enjoy all sorts of transitory physical forms of well-being and comfort. We should not desire any pleasure of this present, mortal and physical life but rather to mourn, bewail and lament our offences, faults and sins without ceasing, and to perfectly despise and annihilate ourselves, and from day to day to be considered more and more abject by others, while in all our insignificance we become worthless even in our own eyes, so that we can be pleasing to God alone, love him alone, and cleave to him alone. We should not wish to be concerned about anything except the Lord Jesus Christ himself who alone should reside in our affections, and we should not be concerned or anxious about anything except him on whose dominion and providence everything in general and individually depends.

So from now on it should not be your aim to seek enjoyment but to truly mourn with all your heart. For that reason, if you do not mourn, mourn for that, while if you do mourn, mourn especially that you have brought the cause of your pain on yourself by your own great offences and infinite sins. For just as a condemned man on receiving his sentence does not concern himself about the seating of the spectators, so he who laments and is genuinely mourning is not interested in pleasures, resentment, fame or wrongs or things of that sort. And just as townsfolk and contemned criminals have different accommodation, the state and position of those who are mourning and have committed offences deserving punishment ought to be completely different from those who are innocent and under no obligation. Otherwise there would be no difference between the guilty and the innocent in matters of punishment and reward. The result would be great dereliction of duty, and evil behaviour would have more freedom than goodness.

So everything must be renounced, everything despised, everything rejected and avoided, so that we can lay a firm foundation of penitent grieving. Then, loving Jesus Christ in reality, yearning for him, and holding him in one's heart, in reality experiencing pain for one's sins and faults, in reality seeking to know the coming Kingdom, while with true faith bearing in mind the reality of the torments and eternal judgement, and firmly and fully taking up the recollection and fear of one's own death, we should be aware of nothing else, and not care or be worried about anything else. For that reason, he who hurries towards the blessed state of impassibility and towards God should reckon himself to have experienced great loss every day that he is not insulted and despised. Impassibility after all is freedom from vices and passions and purity of heart and the adornment of all virtues. So consider yourself as already dead since there is no doubt that you have got to die. And as a final thought let this be the test for you of whether any thought, word or action of yours is of God, whether you are made more humble because of it, more inward and more recollected and established in God. If you find it is otherwise in yourself, you should be suspicious about it, whether it be not according to God, unacceptable to you and not to your benefit.

Proinde, quanto quis vilitatis suae cognitor est, tanto plus et limpidius divinae majestatis est inspector: et quanto aliquis propter Deum, veritatem et justitiam, sibiipsi in oculis suis est vilior, tanto in oculis Dei est pretiosior.

Quapropter studeamus toto desiderii conatu nos vilissimos reputare, et credere indignos omni beneficio, nobis displicere, soli Deo placere, ab aliis indignissimi et vilissimi reputari: insuper super tribulationibus, afflictionibus, et injuriis non moveri, nec super hujusmodi inferentes conturbari, nec cogitationibus contra eos involvi, vel indignari, sed aequo animo credere velis, te cunctis injuriis, vilipensionibus, flagellis, et derelictionibus esse dignum.

Nam re vera, qui vere secundum Deum poenitet et luget, ille ab omnibus honorari ac diligi abhorret, nec subterfugit nec renuit se quodammodo odiri, conculcari, despici, usque in finem, ut vere humilietur, et puro corde soli Domino Deo sincere adhaereat.

Verumtamen ad Dominum Deum solum diligendum, et seipsum super omnia abhorrendum, et ab aliis appetere vilipendi, non requiritur labor extrinsecus, nec corporis valetudo, sed potius solitudo corporis, labor cordis, et quies mentis, ut scilicet labore cordis, et affectione mentis intimae surgat, et corporaliter se ab illis infimis evellat, et sic ad coelestia et divina surgat et ascendat.

Nempe hoc facientes, mutamus nos in Deum: et praecipue tunc fit, quando ex corde eligimus, sine judicio, damnatione et contemptu proximi, nos ut peripsema et opprobrium ab omnibus aestimari, imo ab omnibus tamquam lutum foedum abhorreri, quam quibuscumque deliciis abundare, vel ab hominibus honorari aut elevari, seu qualicumque corporali et transitoria sospitate vel commodo perfrui, nec aliam praesentis hujus mortalitatis et corporalis vitae consolationem desiderare, quam nostras offensiones, culpas, et peccata sine intermissione lugere, deplangere, et plorare, perfecte nos vilipendere et annihilare, et de die in diem ab aliis magis magisque viliores haberi, et in omni vilitate indigni in nostris oculis quotidie fieri, ut soli Deo placeamus, eumque solum diligamus, sicque ei adhaereamus: nec circa aliquid velimus affici, nisi solum circa ipsum Dominum Jesum Christum, qui solus jaceat in nostro affectu: nec de ullo solicitari et curare, nisi de ipso in cujus ditione et providentia universa et singula currunt et subsistunt.

Non ergo tuum erit amodo deliciari, sed vere toto corde lugere. Quamobrem, si non luges, propter hoc luge: si vero luges, propter hoc magis lamentare, quia doloris causam tibi superinduxisti, propter tuas offensiones maximas et peccata infinita. Sicut ergo non sollicitudinem gerit super speculatorum dispositionem, qui sententiam suscipit condemnatus, sic qui lamentatur, et efficaciter luget, neque deliciis, neque irae, aut gloriae, vel indignationi, vel hujusmodi aliquando attendat. Et sicut alia civium, alia sunt damnatorum habitacula, ita lugentium, et habentium ad poenam obligantia delicta, statio et institutio ab innoxiis et non obligatis aliena penitus debet esse et remota. Alioquin non esset differentia rei obnoxii et innocentis, in compensatione et satisfactionis poena, quae tamen magna erat in praevaricationis culpa, et liberior esset injustitia, quam innocentia.

Omnia ergo abneganda, omnia contemnenda, omnia excutienda et vitanda, ut plena fide bonum luctui poenitentiae jaciatur fundamentum. Igitur in veritate Jesum Christum diligens, et post eum lugens, et eum in corde et in corpore portans, in veritate dolorem de suis peccatis et offensionibus habens, in veritate futurum regnum percipere inquirens, necnon in vera fide memoriam tormentorum et judicii aeterni possidens, et sui exitus timorem et memoriam firmiter perfecteque reassumens, non ulterius conabitur, nec curabit, nec sollicitus erit de aliquo alio. Propter quod qui ad beatam impassibilitatem et ad Deum currere festinat, omni die in qua non maledicitur, et contemnitur, se multum damnum arbitretur sustinuisse. Impassibilitas autem est, a vitiis et passionibus libertas, cordis munditia, et virtutum ornatus. Aestima igitur te jam mortuum, quem non ambigis de necessitate moriturum. Et postremum argumentum omnium cogitationum, locutionum, operum tuorum, an secundum Deum sint, sit tibi indicium hoc, videlicet si his magis humilis, et intra te, et in Deo plus recollectus et confortatus fueris. Si autem aliter in te repereris, suspectum tibi sit, ne non sit secundum Deum, nec sibi acceptum, nec tibi proficuum.

How God's Providence includes everything
Providentia Dei, qualiter ad omnia se extendat?

Certainly if we are to come directly, safely and nakedly to our Lord God without hindrance, freely and peacefully, as explained above, and be securely joined to him with even mind in prosperity or adversity, whether in life or in death, then our job is to commit everything unhesitatingly and resolutely, in general and individually, to his unquestionable and infallible providence.

This is hardly surprising since it is he alone who gives to all things their being, their capacity and their action - that is, their strength, operation, nature, manner and order in number, weight and measure. Especially since just as a work of art presupposes a prior operation of nature, in the same way the operation of nature presupposes the work of God, creating, sustaining, ordering and administering it, for to him alone belong infinite power, wisdom, goodness and inherent mercy, justice, truth, love, and unchanging timelessness and omnipresence.

So nothing can exist or act by its own power unless it acts in the power of God himself, who is the prime mover and the first principle, who is the cause of every action, and the actor in every agent. For so far as the nature of the order of things is concerned, God provides for everything without intermediary right down to the last detail. So nothing, from the greatest to the smallest things, can escape God's eternal providence, or fall away from it, whether in matters of the will, of causal events, or even of accidental circumstances outside of one's control. But God cannot do anything which does not fall under the order of his own providence, just as he cannot do anything which is not subject to its operation. Divine providence therefore extends to everything, in general and in particular, even including a man's thoughts. On which subject Scripture has this to say, *Cast all your worries upon him, for he takes care of you.* (1 Peter 5.7) And again the prophet says, *Cast your care upon the Lord, and he will feed you.* (Psalm 55.22) And, *Look at the nations of men, my son, and see that no one ever put his trust in the Lord, and was disappointed. For who has been faithful to his commandments and been abandoned?* (Sirach 2.22) And our Lord himself said, *Do not be anxious, saying, What shall we eat?* (Matthew 6.25) So whatever and however much we can hope from God, we shall undoubtedly receive, as Deuteronomy says, *Every place where you feet tread shall be yours.* (Deuteronomy 11.24) For a man shall receive all that he is able to desire, and so far as he can reach with his foot of faith, even so much shall he possess. That is why Bernard says, "God, the maker of everything is so abounding in mercy that whatever size grace cup of faith we are able to hold out to him, we shall undoubtedly have it filled." And so Mark has it, *All that you ask in prayer believing that you will receive it, will be given you.* (Mark 11.24)

So the stronger and the more vehement our faith in God is, and the more reverently and persistently it is offered up to God, the more surely, the more abundantly and the quicker what we hoped for will be accomplished and obtained.

Indeed if in doing this our faith in God is weak and slow to rise to God on account of the multitude and magnitude of our sins, we should remember this, that everything is possible with God, and that what he wishes is bound to take place, while what he does not wish cannot possibly happen, and that it is as easy for him to forgive and cancel countless sins, however enormous, as to do it with a single sin. While a sinner cannot, of himself, rise from innumerable sins, and free and absolve himself from them, and not even from just one sin. For we are unable not only to do, but even to think anything good, of ourselves, but this is from God.

Nonetheless it is much more dangerous, other things being equal, to be ensnared in many sins than in a single one, since no sin is left unpunished, and every mortal sin deserves infinite punishment, and this by the rigour of justice since any such sin is against God who is indeed worthy of infinite reverence, dignity and honour.

What is more, according to the Apostle Paul, God knows his own (2 Timothy 2.19), and it is impossible for any of them to perish by the whirlwinds and floods of any error, scandal, schism, persecution, heresy, tribulation, adversity or temptation, for he has foreseen from eternity and unchangeably the number of his elect and the extent of their merits in such a way that everything good and bad, what is theirs and not theirs, prosperity and adversity, all work together for them for good, except indeed that they appear even more glorious and commendable in adversity.

So let us commit everything with full assurance, in general and in particular, confidently and unhesitatingly to divine providence, by which God permits however much and whatever sort of evil to happen to us. For it is good and will lead to good, since he permits it to exist, and it would not exist unless he permitted it to exist. Nor could it exist otherwise or more than he permits it to, because he knows how to, has the power to, and wills to change and convert it into something better. For just as it is by operation of providence that all good things exist, so it is by its permission that all bad things are changed into good. In this way in fact God's power, wisdom and mercy are shown forth through Christ our redeemer - his mercy and his justice, the power of grace and the weakness of nature, the beauty of everything in the association of opposites, the approval of the good, and the malice and punishment of the wicked. Similarly the contrition of the converted sinner, his confession, and penitence, the kindness of God, piety, charity and his praise and goodness (all show forth God's power and wisdom). Yet it does not always lead to good in those who do ill, but, as is usually the case, to great danger and extreme evil, in the loss, that is, of grace and their place in glory, and in the incurring of guilt and punishment, sometimes even eternal punishment, from which may Jesus Christ defend us. Amen.

Verumtamen, ut juxta praefata, sine impedimento, expedite, secure et nude in Dominum Deum nostrum libere et tranquille feramur, conjungamur et uniamur, eique firmiter adhaereamus, aequanimiter in prosperis et adversis, in vita sive in morte, opus est ut cuncta et singula indiscussae suae infallibili providentiae indubie committamus et certissime.

Nec mirum, cum ipse solus sit qui omnibus dat esse, posse, et operari, id est, substantiam, virtutem, et operationem, speciem, modum, et ordinem in numero, pondere, et mensura. Praesertim cum sicut opus artis praesupponit opus naturae, ita opus naturae praesupponit opus Dei creantis, conservantis, ordinantis, et administrantis: eo quod ipsius solius sit infinita potentia, sapientia, bonitas, et essentialis misericordia, justitia, et veritas, charitasque, immutabilis aeternitas et immensitas.

Nulla ergo res potest propria virtute subsistere, nec agere, nisi agat in virtute ipsius Dei, scilicet primi moventis, primi principii, qui est causa omnis actionis, et operatur in omni agente. Quippe quantum ad rationem ordinis pertinet, Deus immediate omnibus providet, et usque ad ultima singularia. Nihil igitur a maximo usque ad minimum sempiternam Dei providentiam effugit, nec declinat etiam, sive in voluntariis, sive in causalibus, sive in fortuitis nec de se intentis. Sed nec aliquid Deus facere potest, quin sub ordinem suae providentiae cadat, sicut non potest facere aliquid, quod ejus operationi non subdatur.

Extendit igitur se providentia divina ad omnia et singula, etiam usque ad hominum cogitata. Qua de re Scriptura, juxta illud primae Petri, v.7: *Omnem solicitudinem vestram projicientes in eum, quoniam ipsi cura est de vobis.* Et rursum Propheta: *Jacta super Dominum curam tuam, et ipse te enutriet.* Et, Ecclesiastici, ii. 11 et 12: *Respicite, filii, nationes hominum, et scitote quia nullus speravit in Domino et confusus est. Qui enim permansit in mandatis ejus, et derelictus est?* Et Dominus ait: *Nolite solliciti esse, dicentes: Quid manducabimus?* Quidquid ergo, et quantumcumque magnum a Deo sperare possumus, erimus sine dubio accepturi, secundum illud Deuteronomii, xi.24: *Omnis locus quem calcaverit pes vester, vester erit.* Quia quantumcumque desiderare quis potuerit, tantum est accepturus: et quatenus fiduciae pedem porrexerit, eatenus possidebit. Unde Bernardus: 'Auctor omnium Deus tantae abundat visceribus pietatis, ut ad quantumcumque gratiam fiduciae simum extendere poterimus, tantum erimus sine dubio accepturi.' Unde, Marci, xi. 24: *Omnia quaecumque orantes petitis, credite quia accipietis, et evenient vobis.*

Porro, quanto haec fiducia in Deum fortiorest et instantior, et quanto in Deo cum humilitate et reverentia se violentius erigit, tanto securius, et abundantius, et citius, quod sperabat, impetrabit ac obtinebit.

At vero, si inter haec propter multitudinem et magnitudinem peccatorum fiducia in Deum se erigere tependo retardat, animadvertat qui hujusmodi est, quod omnia possibilia sunt apud Deum: et quod vult, necesse est quod fiat, et quod non vult, impossibile est ut fiat: et quod tam facile est ei tam innumerabilia peccata, quantumcumque enormia, remittere et delere, sicut unum peccatum. Et sicut peccator non potest, quantum in se est, ab innumerabilibus peccatis surgere, et se ab eis executere et absolvere, sic nec ab uno peccato. Non enim possumus non solum facere, sed nec cogitare bonum a nobis, quasi ex nobis, sed hoc ex Deo est.

Attamen utique multo periculosius est, pluribus irretitum esse peccatis, caeteris paribus, quam uno solo: quia nullum malum impunitum, et cuique peccato mortali debetur infinita poena, et hoc de rigore justitiae, eo quod quodlibet tale peccatum sit contra Deum, qui est actu infinitae reverentiae, dignitatis, et honorificentiae.

Praeterea, secundum Apostolum, *cognovit Dominus qui sunt ejus*: et impossibile est aliquem illorum perire, inter quoscumque anfractus et fluctus errorum, scandalorum, schismatum, persecutionum, haeresum, tribulationum, adversitatum, atque tentationum qualiumcumque, eo quod numerus electorum suorum, et terminus meritorum sit aeternaliter et immutabiliter ab eo praevisus, in tantum, ut etiam omnia bona et mala, propria et aliena, prospera et adversa eis cooperentur in bonum, nisi forte in hoc quod gloriosiores et probatiores appareant in adversis.

Secure ergo et expedite cuncta et singula committamus plena cum fiducia divinae providentiae, quae idcirco permittit mala qualiacumque qualitercumque fieri: et bonum est, et bene fit, ut sinat ea fieri: nec fierent nisi permitteret ea fieri: nec aliter nec plus fieri possunt, nisi in quantum permittit, quia scit, potest, et vult ea in melius convertere et disponere. Sicut enim ejus operatione omnia bona fiunt, sic ejus permissione omnia mala bona fiunt: ut certe ex hoc appareat ejus potentia, sapientia, clementia per reparatorem Christum, misericordia et justitia, virtus gratiae, et defectus naturae, pulchritudo universi, comparatione oppositorum, laus bonorum, reproborum malitia atque poena. Similiter in peccatore converso contritio, confessio, et poenitentia, mansuetudo Dei, pietas, et charitas, lausque ejus, et bonitas. Non tamen eis semper cedit in bonum, qui male agunt: sed ut communiter in periculum magnum, et maximum malum, privationis scilicet gratiae et gloriae, et incursionis culpae et poenae, nonnumquam etiam aeternae, a qua nos custodiat Jesus Christus. Amen.